Six-Word Lessons)

BE MORE
PRODUCTIVE

100 Lessons to Increase Focus, Organization and Productivity at Work

Debbie Rosemont

Published by Pacelli Publishing
Bellevue, Washington

Six-Word Lessons to Be More Productive

Copyright © 2009, 2017 by Debbie Rosemont

Published by Pacelli Publishing
9905 Lake Washington Blvd. NE, #D-103
Bellevue, Washington 98004
PacelliPublishing.com

Cover and Interior Design by Pacelli Publishing
Cover photo by Pexels.com via Pixabay
Author photo by Tara Gimmer Photography

ISBN-10: 1-933750-22-7
ISBN-13: 978-1-933750-22-4

L egend has it that Ernest Hemingway was challenged by some friends to write a story in six words. Hemingway responded to the challenge with the following story: *For sale: baby shoes, never worn.*

The story tickles the imagination. Why were the shoes never worn? Were they too small? Did the baby die? Was the baby not able to wear shoes? Any of these are plausible explanations left up to the reader's imagination.

This style of writing has a number of aliases: postcard fiction, flash fiction, micro fiction, and sudden fiction. Lonnie Pacelli, the series creator, was introduced to this style of writing by a friend over a cup of coffee. He was entranced with the idea and started thinking about how this extreme brevity of writing could apply in today's micro-burst communication culture of text messages, tweets, and wall posts. Thus the inspiration for **Six-Word Lessons**.

In **Six-Word Lessons** you will find 100 short, practical tips and ideas to increase your focus, organization, and productivity at work. Rather than pore through pages and pages of content trying to search for what you need, **Six-Word Lessons** gives them to you quickly and easily.

My hope is that you're able to use the ideas from **Six-Word Lessons** to improve your productivity and get more done in less time. Tell me how it's impacted you at story@6wordlessons.com.

Table of Contents

Assess Your Situation, Define Your Goals

1

Why this book? Why right now?

You picked up this book for a reason. Identify what the reason is and why you were drawn to this particular book or topic at this particular time.

Know why you want to increase your organization and productivity. What results do you want?

2

Start with the end in mind.

When you have a goal or vision to work toward it can help clarify the process.

Close your eyes. Imagine what it will be like to be more organized and productive. How will your office look? What will you accomplish? How will you spend your extra time? How will you feel?

3

What specific results do you want?

Write down the specific results you want. Is it to leave the office by 5:00 each day and spend time with your family? Is it to generate additional revenue and if so, how much and by when? Is it to improve customer service? Is it to retain your best employees?

Pick results that will motivate you to implement the lessons in this book. Post them as a reminder to stay on track.

4

Figure out what's holding you back.

What is keeping you from achieving the results you want right now? Is it a disorganized work space? Daily distractions? A difficult time prioritizing? A hard time focusing on your priorities consistently? Poor email or meeting habits?

Knowing what your challenges are can help you decide where to start. Commit to making one change at a time.

5

Take a look around your office.

Assess your current situation. Think about work flow. How do things enter your office? How do they leave? Where do you sit and do most of your work? Are you able to work there, free of distraction?

What's working well in your office right now, and what's not? What can you change in your space to simplify and streamline your work?

6

Share your commitment with someone else.

Choose someone you admire, like and trust. Let them know that you're committed to making a change in your space or in the way you work in order to achieve different results.

Ask them to hold you accountable. Sharing your goals with others greatly increases your chance of success.

13

Organize Your Space, Find Things Fast

7

Ready to organize? Always sort first.

Sort the items to be organized into categories that make sense to you. Put like items together. This will allow you to take inventory of what you have.

Sort and separate supplies, paper, reference materials, marketing materials, equipment, projects, personal items, etc.

See how many of each type of item you have. Decide on how many you need.

16

8

Next step: let go of clutter.

After you've sorted your items and can see what you have as well as define what you need, you're ready to get rid of what you don't need.

Clutter gets in the way of finding what you need, when you need it.

9

Use it? Love it? Need it?

When deciding if something is clutter or not, these can be great questions to ask yourself:

Do you use it often? Do you love it? Do you need it to do your job?

If not, perhaps its time to let it go.

10

Ask: does it add value today?

This is another great question to ask when deciding whether or not to keep something: Is it adding value to your personal or professional life today? (Not did it have value at some point in time, but does it now?)

This goes beyond the monetary value of an item. Is it instrumental to your work or your life? If it's not adding value, it may be detracting. Let it go. Make space.

11

Can you find it somewhere else?

If you're not sure if you can toss something or not, ask yourself, "What's the worst thing that would happen if I needed it again?" Can you find it someplace else? Was it on the internet where you can find it again (or maybe even a more updated version)? Is someone else the primary holder of the information?

Is it something that's easy to replace? If so, let it go.

20

12

If it doesn't fit, toss it.

If an item doesn't fit your current lifestyle or profession, let it go. If it's an article of clothing that literally doesn't fit, let it go.

Make room for the things that serve you well now. Make room for the things you feel great about.

13

Make a decision: keep? toss? donate?

As you go through each item in the categories you've sorted, make decisions.

Is this something to keep, toss or donate? Have some bins nearby as you go through your things. Label them "trash," "recycle." "donate," "goes elsewhere." Things that are "keep" stay out in the area you're working on.

Barbara Hemphill of the Productive Environment Institute says that "Clutter is delayed decisions." Decide.

14

Assign a home to each item.

Everything important in your space should have a specific home. Designate a permanent residence for each item that is a "keep."

When each item has a home, it makes it easier to find it when you need it, and easier to put it away when you're done using it.

15

Consider how you work and move.

When you're assigning a home to the items in your space, you need to think about how you work and move. Are there multiple functions that happen in one space? If so, assign zones.

Are there ergonomic considerations you should keep in mind? Are you right or left handed? Tall? Do you spend a lot of time in one place or move around a lot? Place things around you accordingly.

16

Keep like items with like items.

It's easier to find things when you know that like items are together. When you go looking for a specific supply and it is sometimes here, or sometimes there, it is difficult to know where to look.

On the other hand, when you keep like items together, you know exactly where to look. It's also easier to keep track of your inventory of a certain item and know when you're running low or need to acquire more.

17

Keep things close to where used.

You'll save time and effort when you keep things close to where you use them.

Always take notes when you are on the phone? Keep paper and pen nearby. Is there a particular chair in which you do your reading? Keep reference material, books or periodicals there as well.

Have commonly used work supplies on, in or near your desk. You shouldn't have to get up each time you need to write, staple, cut or compute.

26

18

Use it often? Keep it accessible.

Keep the things you use most often the easiest to get to. The most often used items, files, papers or supplies get the prime real estate.

Things that you use daily should be within arm's reach, either on top of the desk, or in a desk drawer. Things used weekly can be in a filing cabinet right next to your desk. Things used monthly or less frequently can be stored farther away.

27

19

Contain the items you are keeping.

When things have a defined home, it is easier to find them and put them away. When they are contained in some way, they are more likely to stay where you want them. Containers help separate groups of items from one another. Containers can also help you move entire groups of things together.

Containers can be bins, drawers, dividers within drawers, file folders, baskets, or other holders.

20

Use containers to help set boundaries.

Let containers guide you as to how much of something you can/want to keep. For example, do you have lots of magazines? Choose a magazine rack and then only keep the magazines that will fit in that rack. If you have 30 and the rack holds 15, then toss half. Can't decide which? Keep the most current ones. Information in many periodicals tends to be seasonal or time sensitive and gets outdated quickly.

21

Measure your space and stuff first.

Many clients get excited about organizing and run out to buy lots of containers or baskets. Don't do this first! Get containers after you've sorted, cleared clutter and assigned a home to the items you're keeping.

Measure the space where the container will go. Look at the quantity of items it will contain. This way you're sure to find the right container and not end up with container clutter.

22

Use what you have before shopping.

Before you rush out and shop for new containers, take a look around and see if you can use something you already have.

Do you have unused boxes, bins, baskets or other receptacles that can be used for storage now? When they will show, and style matters to you, go ahead and buy what you will need. Won't show? Repurpose a shoe box to hold supplies on a shelf in a cupboard or a checkbook box to act as a drawer divider.

31

23

Clear containers let you see inside.

When it's practical, choose clear containers. You can save time by not having to open them to check contents. Rather, simply peer through the container to instantly know what's inside.

24

Label bins and containers if needed.

Labeling your containers can help you remember where you've put things, what is inside without opening them (especially if they're not clear containers) and make it easier to put things away in the right spot quickly.

An additional benefit to labeling is that it allows someone else to assist you. If you can't be there, someone else can locate items in your office.

Use Systems to Keep it Up

25

Establish habits to help stay organized.

Once you've organized by sorting, clearing clutter, assigning a home and containing your things, you'll want to protect that investment of time by establishing some new habits that will help you stay organized.

If you don't change the behavior that caused the disorganization in the first place, then your space will end up just as it was before in no time at all.

26

After using something, put it away.

It sounds simple and it is. When you are finished using something, put it back in its "assigned home." This will ensure it is there when you need it next time and you won't have to waste time looking everywhere else for the item.

It also keeps your working surface clear of items that aren't currently in use.

27

Before shopping, check your supply first.

Some people buy things unnecessarily and this adds clutter to their spaces. Before you shop, take a look at your current inventory. What do you need? What do you already have?

When things are in their proper "home" it is easy to avoid buying duplicates of things you have but cannot find.

28

Shop mindfully; where will it go?

Before you buy something, know why you're buying it, what purpose it will serve and where it will go. Is it filling a need? Replacing something? Do you have a "home" in mind for it in your space?

If you can't answer "yes" to those questions, think twice about the purchase.

29

New one in, old one out.

Establishing this habit can help you stay in control of your "stuff." When you bring something new into your space, select something that will go out. This will help prevent overcrowding and clutter.

If you want to take it one step further and are trying to simplify your space, when you bring something new in, select two or three items to go out.

30

Purge what you don't need regularly.

Decide that a couple times a year you will go through the organization process again.

Sort, get rid of the things that aren't adding value, decide where to keep the things that are, contain, and establish habits to keep it up.

As new things, paper, projects, etc. continue to come into our lives, we need to do this periodically to stay organized.

31

Schedule time to maintain the organization.

What tasks do you prefer to do daily, weekly, quarterly or annually to maintain the organization?

Perhaps daily you'll clear off your desk. Weekly you'll file the items in your "to file" folder. Monthly you'll commit to reviewing your most active files, quarterly you can purge a reference filing drawer and annually go through your entire office. Schedule that time.

32

Minutes a day keeps clutter away.

At the end of each work day, take a few minutes to return things that you used that day to their proper home. Toss or recycle anything new that came in that you realistically won't read, act on or refer to later. File loose papers on your desk into action or reference files. Take things home that really belong there, and not in your office.

Just a few minutes a day is all it takes.

33

It's a process, not an event.

Organizing isn't something you can just do once and then forget about. Systems and habits like the ones discussed in the previous lessons can help you keep up with the organization.

You'll also want to adjust your organizational systems and review the things around you as you experience change or transition. Make sure that your environment supports your current goals and direction.

Use Your Time Wisely; Maximize Productivity

34

To do, or not to do?

That is the question.

We only have so much time. Use a master "to do" list, or a task list to help you remember all that you want or need to get done.

Each day, select the items off that master list that will bring you closer to your goals.

35

Saying "yes" also means saying "no."

Every time we say "yes" to a request for our time, we are also saying "no" to anything else we might have done with that time.

When you say "yes" to another volunteer position, or another project at work, it may mean you are saying "no" to more time with your family or time for yourself.

Keep the trade-off in mind.

36

Delegate what you can to others.

When you have the resources, delegate what you can to others to free up your time to do the things that only you can do.

If someone else can do a task faster, better or for less money that you bill per hour, it may make sense to off-load the task.

37

Group similar tasks to save time.

Consider chunking tasks like making phone calls, sending emails, working on financials, running errands, or preparing for upcoming clients, meetings or presentations.

When we can "get on a roll" doing one sort of task, it takes less time than it does jumping from one type of task to another and then back again.

38

Block time off on your calendar.

Block time for tasks that need to happen regularly. You may block time on your calendar to get your work-related reading done, filing finished, or client thank-you notes sent.

If you're using an electronic calendar program, like Outlook, you can create these appointments once and then set them to reoccur on your calendar at the frequency you choose (i.e., once a week).

39

Know what time you focus best.

Are you an early morning person and work best when it's quiet in the office? Better after a couple of cups of coffee around 10:00? Really hit your stride in the early afternoon?

Knowing when you "peak" will help you plan your most challenging work for that time. Understand your body's natural rhythm and capitalize on the time when your energy level is highest.

51

40

Let your voicemail work for you.

Phone calls take an average of 12 minutes per call when we answer the phone, and 7 minutes per call when we call out. Know why?

When we place the call, we are in control. We know our agenda and purpose for making the call and can get to the point.

When you're working on high priority tasks, let your voicemail work for you and then return calls in a block of time.

52

Habits Affect Productivity, Good or Bad

41

Prep for tomorrow the night before.

Before you leave the office at the end of the day, review your calendar to see what appointments you have the next day. If you won't come straight to the office first thing, make sure you take with you what you'll need and have directions for any meetings or appointments.

Deciding on your outfit at night can also be a time saver come morning. You'll know that what you need to wear is clean, pressed and ready to go.

42

Utilize a "not to do" list.

What are the low priority tasks you spend time on that keep you from accomplishing your goals? What habits do not serve you well? What do you busy yourself with in order to procrastinate?

Make a list of the things you'd like to stop doing and post it somewhere visible. Know that when you stop doing things on this list you'll get some real work done!

43

Leave the day after vacation open.

Do you usually return from vacation and jump right back in to meetings, client appointments and rushing from one thing to another? If you do, it probably feels like it takes a long time to get "caught up" and it can negate some of the R & R from your time away.

Leave the day you return to work open to get through voicemail, email, snail mail, process items in your inbox and get back in the groove. You'll be glad you did.

44

Use one calendar for all scheduling.

Keep work and personal appointments on one calendar so that you can see all of your commitments at once.

This can help you avoid scheduling an evening meeting on your son's birthday, or a dentist appointment on the day of an important deadline for your department. It can also help you not over-commit when you see all that is going on for a certain day, week or month.

45

Multi-tasking really doesn't work; focus instead.

When we try to do two things at the same time it takes us longer than if we had focused on one at a time. We're asking our brain to switch from one task to another and we lose time this way. The chance of errors also increases as our attention is divided.

It is far more efficient to focus. Complete one task and then move on to another.

46

Eliminate all distraction to stay focused.

We are often distracted from a task at hand by a "shiny object." Something, sometimes *anything*, that catches our attention.

Clear clutter off your desk. Step away from the computer if you're not using it on your project. Turn the ringer off on your phone. Close your office door if you're able. Now focus.

47

Get the hardest thing done first.

If you tend to procrastinate on priority work, try getting the tough task out of the way. Tackling something big first or "eating a frog for breakfast," as author Brian Tracy says, can do two things.

First, it can give you a great sense of accomplishment for the rest of the day. Second, it gives you momentum to keep on going. You may find you get more done in less time by doing the hard thing first.

Plan Your Work, Work Your Plan

48

Use a planner - paper or electronic.

It doesn't have to be fancy. Simple is fine. Use a planner. Use it to keep track of your appointments, commitments, contacts, and notes. Having all of these things in once place is invaluable.

Chose a planner that you are comfortable using and that can be portable. Use it daily. It's stressful to try to remember everything. Write things down or capture them in your planner and reduce stress.

49

Write down your goals, review regularly.

Committing goals to paper can make them seem more real. Writing them down also means you don't have to remember them in your brain. They are on paper for you to refer to, to plan for and to review regularly.

Review your goals periodically to help you set priorities for your tasks (they should relate to your goals) and to adjust them as time passes or as needed.

50

Create action plans to achieve goals.

Once you have your goals written, make a plan. How will you achieve the goal? Is anyone else involved? Do you need to do any preparation before you begin working toward the goal? What projects need to be accomplished to reach the goal?

Create a plan. Know how it will get done.

51

Break your projects into specific tasks.

What steps do you need to take to implement your action plan and complete the project at hand? What will you do first? Second? Last?

Break your project down into specific, actionable tasks. A long term project on its own might seem overwhelming, but a single task can seem reasonable. Accomplish your project one task at a time.

52

If it's important, schedule it in.

Don't let your day "happen to you." Plan it out. If you have things you want to accomplish, make an appointment with yourself to get them done.

Schedule time on your calendar to work on priority tasks, just as you would schedule time for a client or a meeting. Honor and protect that time.

53

Work for 50, break for 10.

In each hour, work hard for 50 minutes and then take a 10-minute break to do something enjoyable. Treat this time as your "reward" for staying focused.

Use the break to truly break from work. Take a brisk walk, get a cup of tea, call a friend, use a social networking site for fun. When you return to work after the break, you'll be re-energized and ready to produce again.

54

Apply the 80/20 rule at work.

Pareto's Principle states that we get 80 percent of our results from 20 percent of our effort. What is your 20 percent that makes the biggest difference in your work? Do more of that.

Identify what the 80 percent (less effective) tasks are and find ways to reduce, delegate, or eliminate them to have more time to spend on the 20 percent that really matters.

55

Work from home? Compartmentalize your day.

It may be tempting if you work from home to switch back and forth from work to personal tasks throughout the day. After all, isn't that one of the benefits of your situation?

While this may allow for great flexibility, it may not be the most efficient way to work. Compartmentalizing tasks will provide more structure, and allow you to get more done in less time.

56

Share your plan with someone else.

When you share your goals and plan with someone else you increase your chance of success in executing your plan and reaching your goals.

Knowing that someone else knows what you're working on motivates you to actually work on it. That person may ask you about your progress and may serve as a sounding board or resource should you run into any barriers.

57

It's okay to ask for help.

If you get stalled or stuck while working your plan, reach out for some assistance. You may need a pep talk, some direction, or possibly some help in doing the work.

If you don't ask, you may not get out of the rut. If the end result is still important, do what you can to make it a reality. Get help when you need it to move forward again.

58

Pair up with an accountability partner.

An accountability partner can not only hold you accountable for what you say you want to accomplish, but can also brainstorm with you to generate new ideas, problem solve with you to overcome obstacles, collaborate on projects, and celebrate your success.

Consider meeting by phone at regular intervals to report on goals and commit to next actions.

59

Perfectionism can be paralyzing to productivity.

Perfectionism is the number one cause for procrastination. Perfectionists have a hard time starting something, and a hard time finishing it, because they worry that they can't do it perfectly.

If this is you, recognize it and work to buck your perfectionist tendencies. As the Nike slogan says "Just do it."

60

Remember, done is better than perfect.

Do you really want it done, or do you want it perfect? Decide that done is better than perfect. When we wait for perfect, sometimes tasks never get done.

Do a task well enough and then move on. You'll save time and resources to get more done when you don't spend them on perfecting the last 5 percent of a project.

61

If you procrastinate, find out why.

We procrastinate for several reasons. A few of the most common are a fear of failure, a lack of clarity on what we should do (or what we should do first), a false belief that we work better under pressure or because we really dislike a task and would rather not spend time on it.

Identify why you are putting something off and then you can do something about it (get clarity, delegate, decide "done is better than perfect," or just get started).

62

Start your day by reviewing priorities.

When we fill a jar with sand and pebbles, it's hard to get big rocks in. When we put the big rocks in first, then the pebbles and sand filter though and more can fit in the jar.

What are your big rocks for the day? Review your priorities and make a plan so that your day doesn't get filled with the sand and pebbles, leaving no room for the rocks.

63

Which tasks will make the difference?

To identify what your big rocks are for the day, take a quick look at the goals you have posted. Which tasks on your "to do" list will move you closer to one of your goals?

If you could only accomplish one thing today, what is the one thing that would make the biggest difference in your work, for your business, or your life? That is your top priority for the day.

Six-Word Lessons to Be More Productive

Manage Email or It'll Manage You

64

Do one big thing before email.

Julie Morgenstern wrote a book titled "Never Check Email in the Morning." The premise of the book was that many people jump right on email at the start of their work day and then never get off. They only react to what's coming in.

If you want to be proactive instead of reactive with your work, try getting your most important task done before even checking your email.

65

Check email intermittently, not all day.

Instead of allowing email to create interruptions to the other work you're doing all throughout the day, decide on certain times you'll check email to see if anything requires response or action.

This may be once every 30 minutes, once an hour, every other hour, or possibly just a few times a day. Focus on your priorities in between, instead of constantly flipping back and forth.

66

Process email several times each day.

Processing email is different than checking email. Instead of checking email throughout the day, scan it periodically (maybe hourly) to see if there's anything you need to respond to immediately, then wait to process your email in chunks.

You might try processing your email at 10:00, 1:00 and 4:00 daily (or whatever times work best for you).

67

Make a decision on each email.

When you process your email, you're doing much more than "checking it" or even "reading it." You're making a decision on each email and removing each one from your inbox.

Delete, forward, quickly reply, file for future reference or put in an action file for follow up later. Make a decision.

68

Clear your inbox daily or weekly.

If you have not been in the habit of completely processing your email on a regular basis you may have hundreds or even thousands sitting in your inbox right now.

Take some time to do an "inbox detox" and clear it out. Set up systems so that you can confidently move emails out of your inbox. This may take several sessions and some dedicated time.

Once you've invested that time, keep it up at least weekly, if not daily.

69

Widen your "Send and Receive" sweep.

To remove the temptation of checking email all throughout the day, you may benefit by widening your "Send/Receive Sweep." This is the interval at which emails are swept into your inbox from your ISP or server. The default setting is to have emails come into your inbox as they arrive. Instead, you can change this interval (to every 60 minutes, for example) in the Send/Receive settings.

70

Turn off visual and audio notifiers.

It's a shiny object. A distraction.

If you have a visual or auditory indicator each time a new email comes into your inbox, it draws your attention away from what you are working on at the moment. It takes time for you to redirect your attention again. Additionally, you may be tempted to go check the new email, also taking your concentration away from what you were working on. Do this all day long, and you're wasting a lot of time. Turn them off.

71

Send fewer emails, receive fewer emails.

For every five emails you receive, roughly three will require a response. That means that for every five emails you send, you'll get three back. If you want to receive fewer emails in your inbox, send fewer.

Unsubscribe to any email newsletters you receive but don't read. Let those in your network know that you don't care for "chain" email (i.e., "read this and pass it on for good luck"). Model the type of email you do appreciate receiving (necessary, targeted, clear, to the point).

72

Use rules and filters for email.

Do you routinely receive email that you know you'll look at later as you have time, or that you don't need to read at all but must keep for reference? You can set rules and filters to keep them out of your inbox.

Look for "Tools" and then "Rules" to set filters that will work for you. This is another effective option for maintaining control over your inbox.

73

Email is both sticky and slippery.

After we send an email, we don't have control of its fate. We know who we send it to, but we don't know what they will do with it from there. Email is written documentation. It can be forwarded at the will of the receiver. This makes email both sticky and slippery.

Make sure that what you send in email is relevant, appropriate, and something you wouldn't mind seeing on the front page of the newspaper.

74

Craft emails that are easily read.

There are a number of techniques you can use to send stronger emails. Using these techniques can also model to others the type of email you'd like to receive.

Be clear and to the point. Use bullet points. Break up large blocks of text into shorter paragraphs so there is more white space on the screen. Don't try to cover too many subjects in one email. Separate out any call to action. Let the receiver know what you want them to do.

75

Ensure it's the best communication channel.

Sometimes email isn't the best way to communicate. Sensitive information may be better discussed in person. Complex discussions with large groups of people may be hashed out more effectively in a meeting. Scheduling requests are often handled more efficiently via phone.

Think about what you're trying to accomplish and decide if email is the best way to go before you hit send.

76

Be clear in your subject line.

A clear subject line can go a long way in creating an effective email. Let the receiver know what to expect or what to do with the email. Sometimes a subject line is all you need. In that case, close your subject line with (EOM), meaning "end of message." For example, "Meeting rescheduled for 12/15 at 2:00 (EOM)."

You can also use terms like "Delivery: Monthly report" or "Action: Respond to survey by Friday at noon."

77

Use "reply all" and "cc:" judiciously.

Remember the statistic about the number of emails you send and the resulting number of emails you'll receive? Keep this in mind before you "reply all" or "cc:" people in emails. Do they really need to receive the email you're sending?

Target the right people. Send to those that will find your email relevant and informative. Reply only to the sender if your response only impacts them.

We've Gotta Stop
Meeting Like This

78

Ask: Do we need to meet?

Before deciding to meet in person, determine if the meeting is needed. Know your purpose. Can the same objectives be accomplished by phone or email? This is especially important when there is travel time involved.

Do you meet weekly simply out of habit or because "we've always done it that way"? Make sure that the meeting will be productive and if not, don't meet just for the sake of meeting.

79

Invite the right people to meetings.

Ask people to attend who have something to contribute, are decision makers or need the information.

People who don't fit these categories will make better use of their time, and your meeting will be more effective, if they stay back and accomplish other work.

80

Distribute an agenda, stick to it.

Send out an agenda ahead of time and follow it during the meeting. This lets people know what to expect out of the meeting, to be prepared with any material or information they'll need to contribute, and can help the meeting stay on track so you accomplish what you intended in the allotted time.

You'll know where to start, what topic follows another, and where to conclude.

81

Ask participants to do their homework.

When you distribute an agenda, participants will know what will be covered in the meeting. If they are to deliver a report, give an update, or be ready to discuss materials you've sent out ahead of time, make sure to set the expectation that people come prepared, having read any relevant material, and ready to present or discuss as warranted.

This preparation will help you make the best use of the time spent in the meeting.

99

82

Get off track? Use parking lot.

If discussion gets off track, or new topics come up that are not on the agenda, ask a scribe to record them, so they can be captured and addressed at a later date. "Park them" for future conversation.

This can ensure participants feel "heard" and that off-topic but important issues are not forgotten. It also allows you to stick to the agenda and accomplish the objectives already on the table during the time of your meeting.

100

83

No side conversations allowed; it's distracting.

Ask participants to be fully present during meetings and not engage in side conversations. These side conversations can be distracting both to whoever is speaking as well as to those trying to listen. Additionally, those involved in the side conversation may miss out on important information discussed by the group.

84

Go topless. No, not that kind!

Laptop-less. Unless they're needed for note-taking or for pulling reports or documents relevant to the meeting.

Discourage participants from checking email, surfing the internet, or otherwise using electronic devices such as laptops or hand held technology. You will maximize the effectiveness of your meetings when all participants are fully present and engaged.

85

Assigning action to individuals creates ownership.

When decisions are made and follow-up work will be required, decide who will be accountable, when action will be taken and how they will report back to the group.

Not taking these steps could result in a lack of ownership on everyone's part and wasted time during the meeting.

86

Start and end meetings on time.

When you consistently start and end meetings on time, you teach people that you respect their time, and ask that they respect yours.

Starting meetings late punishes those who are on time. It teaches people that they can come late and it just won't matter. You'll find that people will start coming later and later. Ending meetings late makes participants anxious and causes them to lose focus. Start and end on time.

87

As you conclude, sum it up.

It can be helpful at the end of a meeting to briefly review the topics covered, decisions made, follow-up tasks assigned and any other next actions. Make sure all participants are on the same page and bring closure to the meeting.

Let the group know when you will meet again and ask that they add the date and time to their calendars right away.

88

Leave transition time after each meeting.

When you return to your office after a meeting, take time to file away meeting notes, schedule next actions needed onto your calendar, mark the date and time of the next meeting, and put away any other related files or supplies you brought back with you or had out for the meeting.

When we rush from one meeting to another, or just dump things on our desk after meetings "for now," then clutter ensues. Take the time to put things away.

106

The Paperless Society that Never Was

89

It's important to organize your paper.

Despite the push for the paperless society that started several decades ago, we have more paper in our lives now than ever before. It's here to stay. More comes in each day. If we want to find it when we need it, and act on it when appropriate, then we need systems to deal with it.

90

Average worker wastes six weeks annually.

According to the Wall Street Journal, the average American worker wastes at hour a day looking for paper or information they know they have but cannot find. That equates to six weeks per year.

Use a system for your paper and information that works for you. Invest time in creating your system and you will realize the return on that investment again and again.

91

Out of sight, out of mind?

The average worker has 37 hours of unfinished work on their desk at any one time. Do you keep all of your paper out on your desk because you worry that if you put it away, you'll forget to act on it?

If you have a system you can rely on to store your papers, and "tickle" your memory when its time to act on them, you don't need to have it all out in front of you.

File papers away so that you can work on the task at hand free of distraction.

92

Use an effective action filing system.

File papers by *when* you intend to act (commonly called a "tickler filing system") or by *what* you intend to do (also known as a categorical filing system).

Either way, make sure to build in a system to remind you when to act on certain papers or perform certain tasks. With a tickler system, the structure of the system itself will remind you. With a categorical system, you may also want coordinating prompts on your calendar.

93

Use an effective reference filing system.

Set up a system to keep papers you don't need to act on, but may need to refer to at a later date, or need to keep for regulatory purposes.

Keep like papers together by creating logical broad categories and sub-categories for your work.

Label files and folders clearly with names you'll think of when you go to find the information in the future.

94

Don't overstuff your file drawers.

Make sure your file drawers have some "breathing room" in them. If drawers or files are overstuffed, it is difficult, sometimes even physically painful, to add papers or files. When something is difficult, we are far less likely to do it.

95

Open mail daily over recycling bin.

A lot of the paper we receive each day can be tossed or recycled. Make it a habit to open your mail or review new papers received into your inbox each day with a recycle bin right by your side.

Immediately toss junk mail, unsolicited information that you don't need, or other paper you won't act on or refer to.

96

Shred all paper containing sensitive information.

Shred paper you no longer need that contains information you wouldn't want to get into the hands of others. This might include personal information, financial information, account numbers, personnel records, client files, or other sensitive information.

Use a cross-cut shredder and properly dispose of the information.

97

Weed out your office files regularly.

Weed out your files regularly to get rid of things you no longer need and create space for new things to come.

Schedule periodic appointments with yourself to accomplish this task. It may be that you choose to do one drawer per month or quarter, or your whole system at the end of each year.

98

Stop and think before you print.

Go paperless where you can. Consider the environment, your filing system and your work space before you print something out.

Ask yourself if you really need a paper copy of the document. Would it be easy to find online again? Can you store it electronically? If it is reference material, will it be outdated soon anyway and you'll need to replace it with new information?

99

Have electronic files mirror paper files.

Utilize the same categories and subcategories for your electronic files as you do for your paper files. This makes it easier to find things in both places. It is easier to remember one filing structure than two. It can also make it easier for someone else to step in and help you in your absence.

And Number 100...

100

Use systems and habits that work!

Systems and habits will help you stay organized and be as productive as you can. They will ensure that you stay focused on high priority tasks so you get more of the important things done in the time you have.

Use them to increase revenue, save time and reduce stress. They make work (and life!) easier.

See the entire Six-Word Lesson Series at *6wordlessons.com*

Want more great organization and productivity resources? Check out *itssimplyplaced.com*

Made in the USA
San Bernardino, CA
27 August 2017